HOW TO STRENGTHEN YOUR FAITH IN DIFFICULT TIMES

Tips for Overcoming Challenges and Maintaining a Positive Outlook

Xavier Benedict

COPYRIGHT PAGE

Table of Contents

Introduction

In times of uncertainty and adversity, it is easy to lose faith in ourselves and the world around us. However, it is precisely in these difficult times that it is most important to have a positive outlook and strengthen our faith in ourselves and others. In this book, we offer you some tips to help you stay positive and overcome any challenges that may arise.

Chapter 1

Understanding Faith in Difficult Times

Faith serves as an anchor during difficult times, providing hope, strength, and a sense of purpose. It is in these challenging moments that faith is tested and has the opportunity to grow stronger (Cordero, 2021). By seeking support from a supportive community and developing effective coping skills, individuals can cultivate the resilience needed to navigate through adversity. Additionally, spiritual practices such as prayer, meditation, and reflection can bring a sense of peace and guidance during difficult times.

Nonetheless, bolstering psychological resilience should be a primary public health emphasis during the COVID-19 pandemic. Social support from family, friends, and a special caring loved one were each independently associated with greater resilience in our sample. During periods of shelter-in-place orders, it is important to foster these relationships and to find creative ways to stay emotionally connected with those we care about.

Daily activities are also important in strengthening faith during difficult times. Engaging in activities that bring joy and purpose, such as spending time in nature, exercising, or pursuing hobbies, can uplift the spirit and reinforce one's sense of faith. Moreover, maintaining a positive mindset and reframing challenges as opportunities for growth can also strengthen one's faith in difficult times. By relying on the support of a community and engaging in spiritual practices, individuals can strengthen their faith in challenging times. Despite the widespread yet erroneous belief that people need only draw upon some heroic strength of character, science now tells us that it is the reliable presence of at least one supportive relationship and multiple opportunities for developing effective coping skills that are the essential building blocks for strengthening the capacity to do well in the face of significant adversity. Religious faith can have a positive influence on emotions and may be directly related to improved functional ability. Disciplines of faith, such as solitude, silence, and meditation, may promote mental health and provide a sense of peace. Additionally, seeking guidance and wisdom from spiritual leaders or mentors can provide insights and encouragement in strengthening one's faith.

Chapter 2

Cultivating Strong Beliefs

Beliefs are like the building blocks of our faith. They're the ideas and principles we hold onto tightly, shaping how we see the world and guiding our actions. In this chapter, we'll talk about how to make our beliefs sturdy and resilient, so they can support us through tough times.

Getting to Know Your Core Beliefs

Start by thinking about what you truly believe in. What values and ideas are most important to you?

Reflect on how these beliefs give your life meaning and direction, especially when things get tough.

Finding Strength in Your Faith Tradition

Take a closer look at the teachings and stories from your faith. What wisdom do they offer for dealing with hard times?

Seek advice from people in your faith community who have faced challenges and remained strong in their beliefs.

Ways to Strengthen Your Beliefs

Practice habits that reinforce what you believe. This could be praying, meditating, or reading scriptures regularly.

Surround yourself with supportive friends and family who share your beliefs and can encourage you when times are hard.

Being Open to Growth and Change

Remember that it's okay for your beliefs to evolve. Sometimes new experiences or insights can challenge what you thought you knew.

Stay curious and willing to explore different perspectives,

even if they don't align perfectly with what you've always believed.

Finding Meaning and Purpose in Your Beliefs

Think about how your beliefs help you make sense of difficult situations. Do they give you a sense of purpose or help you find meaning in suffering?

Consider how your beliefs influence the way you live your life and treat others. Do they inspire you to be kind, compassionate, and resilient?

Chapter 3

Nurturing Your Faith Every Day

In this chapter, we're going to talk about simple things you can do every day to strengthen your faith. These practices can help you feel more connected to your beliefs and find comfort and guidance in difficult times.

Make Time for Prayer or Meditation

Set aside a few minutes each day to pray or meditate. It doesn't have to be long or complicated –

just a quiet moment to connect with your faith.

Use this time to talk to your higher power, express gratitude, or simply quiet your mind and listen for guidance.

Read or Reflect on Sacred Texts

Spend some time reading from your faith's sacred texts, whether it's the Bible, Quran, Torah, or another religious book.

Reflect on the teachings and stories you read, and think about how they apply to your own life and struggles.

Practice Acts of Kindness and Compassion

Look for opportunities to show kindness and compassion to others throughout your day. It could be as simple as smiling at a stranger or offering a listening ear to a friend in need.

By living out your faith through acts of kindness, you'll not only strengthen your own beliefs but also make the world a better place.

Find Community and Support

Surround yourself with others who share your faith and values. This could be through attending religious services, joining a faith-based community group, or participating in online forums or social media groups.

Being part of a supportive community can provide encouragement, accountability, and a sense of belonging.

Spend Time in Nature

Take time to appreciate the beauty and wonder of the natural world around you. Whether it's a walk in the park, a hike in the mountains, or simply sitting outside and watching the sunset, spending time in nature can be a deeply spiritual experience.

Use this time to connect with your higher power and reflect on the awe and majesty of creation.

Practice Gratitude

Cultivate an attitude of gratitude by taking time each day to count your blessings and express appreciation for the good things in your life.

Even amid challenges, there are always things to be grateful for. By focusing on the positive, you can shift your perspective and find hope and joy in difficult times.

Chapter 4

Building Supportive Communities

In this chapter, we'll talk about the importance of surrounding yourself with people who share your faith and values. These supportive communities can provide encouragement, strength, and a sense of belonging, especially during difficult times.

Attend Religious Services or Gatherings

Make an effort to attend religious services or gatherings regularly, whether it's a weekly church service, mosque prayer, synagogue gathering, or another form of worship.

Being part of a community of believers can offer comfort, inspiration, and a sense of unity with others who share your faith.

Join Faith-Based Groups or Organizations

Look for opportunities to get involved in faith-based groups or organizations in your community. This could include Bible study groups, prayer circles, or volunteer groups that serve those in need.

These groups can provide a sense of camaraderie and support, as well as opportunities for spiritual growth and service.

Seek Out Online Communities and Resources

In addition to in-person gatherings, consider joining online communities or forums where you can connect with others who share your faith. This could be through social media groups, online forums, or religious websites.

Online communities can offer support, encouragement, and a sense of connection, especially for those who may not have access to a physical faith community in their area.

Foster Meaningful Relationships

Take time to cultivate meaningful relationships with fellow believers. This could involve reaching out to members of your faith community, attending social events or gatherings, or participating in small group discussions.

Building strong relationships with others who share your faith can provide a sense of support, companionship, and understanding during both good times and bad.

Be a Source of Support for Others

Offer support and encouragement to others in your faith community who may be going through difficult times. This could involve listening nonjudgmentally, offering practical help or assistance, or simply being present and offering a word of comfort or prayer.

By being a source of support for others, you not only strengthen your faith but also contribute to the strength and resilience of your faith community as a whole.

Chapter 5

Embracing Growth and Strength

When we face challenges in life, it's natural to feel overwhelmed, discouraged, or even defeated. However, these challenges can serve as catalysts for personal growth and a deeper connection to our faith. Instead of viewing difficult times as insurmountable obstacles, we can choose to see them as opportunities for learning, strength-building, and spiritual development.

Here's a breakdown of how facing challenges can lead to personal growth and a deeper sense of faith:

Understanding the Transformative Power of Adversity

Recognize that facing adversity is a natural part of life and can lead to personal growth and resilience.

Instead of seeing challenges as obstacles to overcome, view them as opportunities for learning and self-discovery.

Cultivating Resilience and Adaptability

Develop resilience by learning to bounce back from setbacks and failures. This involves developing coping skills, practicing self-care, and seeking support from others.

Embrace adaptability by being open to change and willing to learn from new experiences. Flexibility and adaptability are key traits that can help us navigate difficult times with grace and resilience.

Finding Meaning and Purpose in Suffering

Instead of viewing suffering as meaningless or unjust, seek to find purpose and meaning in your struggles.

Reflect on how facing challenges has shaped your character, strengthened your faith, and deepened your sense of empathy and compassion for others.

Seeking Support and Guidance

Don't be afraid to reach out for support when you're facing difficult times. Whether it's from friends, family, or members of your faith community, seeking help is a sign of strength, not weakness.

Consider seeking guidance from a spiritual leader or counselor who can provide wisdom, support, and guidance during challenging times.

Embracing Hope and Resilience

Remember that difficult times are temporary, and there is always hope for a brighter future.

Cultivate resilience by focusing on the things you can control, practicing gratitude, and staying connected to your faith and supportive community.

Chapter 6

Strategies for Overcoming Challenges and Keeping a Positive Attitude

Learn to manage stress

Stress can cause us to lose perspective and self-confidence. To maintain a positive attitude, it is important to learn how to manage stress effectively. Try relaxation techniques such as meditation, yoga, or deep breathing, and seek support from friends, family, or a therapist if you feel you need additional help.

Maintain a healthy routine

Maintaining a healthy routine is essential to maintaining a positive attitude and strengthening our faith in ourselves. Try to get enough sleep each night, exercise regularly, and eat a balanced, nutritious diet. These small actions can make a big difference in our mental and physical health.

Find motivation in your goals

Having clear and achievable goals can be a **source of motivation** and self-belief. Make a list of your goals and work towards them little by little. Celebrate every small success and remember that every step you take brings you closer to your goals.

Seek inspiration from others

Seeking inspiration from others can help us maintain a positive outlook and strengthen our faith in humanity. Read success stories, talk to people you admire, and find online communities or support groups that share your values and goals. Support and inspiration from others can be a source of motivation and faith in ourselves and others.

Find meaning in your life

Finding meaning and purpose in our lives can be essential to maintaining a positive attitude and strengthening our faith in ourselves. Ask yourself what your values are and what you are passionate about in life. Then, look for ways to integrate these elements into your everyday life. You can find meaning and purpose at work, in volunteer activities, in creative hobbies, or in meaningful relationships with friends and family.

Practice gratitude

Gratitude is a powerful tool for maintaining a positive outlook and strengthening our faith in ourselves and others. Every day, take a few minutes to reflect on the things you are grateful for. They can be small things, like a hot cup of coffee in the morning, or bigger things, like having loving people in your life. Practicing gratitude regularly can help you maintain a positive outlook and appreciate what you have instead of focusing on what you lack.

Accept failure as part of the learning process

Failure can be difficult to accept, but it is a natural part of the learning process and strengthening our faith in ourselves. Instead of focusing on the failure itself, focus on what you can learn from the situation and how you can use that experience to grow and move forward. Remember that failure is not a sign that you are incapable or unworthy of success, but simply a part of the path toward your goals.

Maintain a positive attitude in the face of challenges

Maintaining a positive attitude in the face of challenges can be instrumental in maintaining a positive outlook and strengthening our faith in ourselves. Instead of focusing on what could go wrong, focus on the opportunities that present themselves and how you can grow and learn from the challenges. Remember that every challenge you face is an opportunity to strengthen your faith in yourself and your ability to overcome obstacles.

Seek help if you need it

Don't be afraid to seek help if you feel you need additional support to stay positive and strengthen your belief in yourself. Talk to trusted friends or family, seek therapy or support online, or join a support group that focuses on your interests and needs. Remember that asking for help is not a sign of weakness, but rather a sign of strength and resilience to seek the help you need to overcome any challenge you may face.

Conclusion

Throughout this book, we've explored practical strategies and timeless principles for navigating difficult times with faith and resilience. We've learned the importance of grounding ourselves in core beliefs, nurturing spiritual practices, building supportive communities, and embracing growth and strength in the face of adversity.

Ultimately, our faith is like a sturdy anchor that keeps us grounded when the storms of life rage around us. By cultivating a deeper connection to our beliefs, surrounding ourselves with supportive communities, and embracing challenges as opportunities for growth, we can strengthen our faith and emerge from difficult times with greater resilience, wisdom, and spiritual depth.

As we continue on our journey, may we remember that we are not alone. We have the support of our faith community, the guidance of our beliefs, and the strength of our inner resilience to carry us through even the darkest of times. With faith as our guide, we can face whatever challenges come our way with courage, grace, and hope for a brighter tomorrow.

The End

www.ingramcontent.com/pod-product-compliance
Lightning Source LLC
LaVergne TN
LVHW020528160826
845677LV00015B/3971

* 9 7 9 8 8 8 2 1 5 0 6 4 7 *